I0170287

1

ABC'S OF ANIMALS

ABC'S OF ANIMALS

ABC'S OF ANIMALS

ABC'S OF ANIMALS

ABC'S OF ANIMALS

ABC'S OF ANIMALS

ABC'S OF ANIMALS

ABC'S OF ANIMALS

ABC'S OF ANIMALS

ABC'S OF ANIMALS

ABC'S OF ANIMALS

ABC'S OF ANIMALS

LIONS, DISCOVER THE SECOND LARGEST LIVING CAT AFTER THE TIGER.

ABC'S OF ANIMALS

ABC'S OF ANIMALS

Pamela Brown

Author, Publisher, Editor & Illustrator

Direct Contact: Pamela Brown,

Books Speak For You Publications

267-454-3317

Pamelainthelight@yahoo.com

Booksspeakforyou@yahoo.com

Pamelainthelight Publications.com

BooksSpeakForYou.com

Copyright © 2015 Pamela Brown

All rights reserved. No part of this book may be used or reproduced by any means, graphic, electronic, or mechanical, including photocopying, recording, taping or by any information storage retrieval system without the written permission of the publisher except in the case of brief quotations embodied in critical articles and reviews.

Pamelainthelight Publications/Books Speak For You books may be ordered through booksellers or by contacting:

Books Speak For You
A Division Of Pamelainthelight Publications
Philadelphia, PA
Booksspeakforyou.com
Pamelainthelight.com
267-454-3317
The views expressed in this work are solely those of the author.
Any illustration provided by iStock and such images are being used for illustrative purposes.
Certain stock imagery © iStock.
ISBN: 978-1-943611-12-6
Library of Congress Control Number: 2015912537
Printed in the United States Of America

BOOKS SPEAK FOR YOU
A Division of Pamelainthelight Publications

ACKNOWLEDGEMENT

I would like to acknowledge God for all the gifts He has bestowed upon me.

Without God I would not exist. I am nothing without God.

God is the reason for my existence and it is through the Spirit of Jesus that I am able to create and produce the literary material that I produce.

Thank You Lord.

DEDICATION

I dedicate this book to my Mother, Queen Brown, my children, Carrayah Queen-Ella, Gabriel Joel & Carrynn Erin-Josette, my nephews, Jonah, Noah, Marcus-Judah & Joshia, Jonathan Walker CEO and Founder of Project, Men Of Distinction of The J. L. Walker Project, parents, guardians, mothers, fathers, teachers, librarians, therapist, counselors, pediatricians, principals and every person that has anything to do with the fortifying and cultivation of children in the world.

Continue to let your light shine in the lives of children just as God allows His Light To Shine in the Sun, which sits in the sky and His Son, who Shines In Our Lives.

Be Blessed

INTRODUCTION

ABC's Of Animals is a book listing the names and certain facts about animals in alphabetical order.

A is for Alpaca

LOOK, SEE, and read the facts', exploring is where it's at:

Alpacas are domesticated; they have been for thousands of years. Alpacas are bred mainly for their thick fibrous fleece. Alpacas are related to camels and are thought to have Vicuna ancestry. Alpacas are trainable, very smart and come in 22 natural colors. Alpacas are found on almost every continent.

B is for Bushbaby

LOOK, SEE, and read the facts', exploring is where it's at:

Bushbabies have excellent jumping abilities. Bushbabies eat insects, eggs fruit and small animals. Bushbabies are native to Africa. Bushbabies have strong toes, which help them with climbing and they are nocturnal. (Nocturnal –active mainly during the night).

C is Curlew,

LOOK, SEE, and read the facts', exploring is where it's at:

Curlews are a group of eight species of birds, characterized by long, slender, down curved bills and mottled broom plumage. They are one of the most ancient lineages of scolopacid waders. Curlews feed on mud or very soft ground, searching for worms and other invertebrates with their long bills.

D is for Dingo

LOOK, SEE, and read the facts', exploring is where it's at:

Dingos are native to Australia. Dingos natural habitat includes grasslands or deserts. Dingos are also canines.

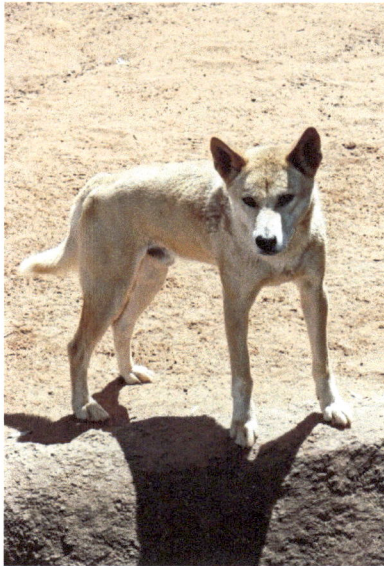

E is for Echidna

LOOK, SEE, and read the facts', exploring is where it's at:

Echidnas eat ants and termites. There are four species of Echidna. Echidnas are egg laying mammals.

F is for Fennec Fox

LOOK, SEE, and read the facts', exploring is where it's at:

The Fennec Fox is the smallest of the foxes. An adult fennec fox weighs 2 pounds and is identified by their very large ears. Fennec Fox help reduce the rodent and locust population.

G is for Gnu

LOOK, SEE, and read the facts', exploring is where it's at:

Gnu's are also called Wildebeest. Gnu's can go 5 days without water. Gnu's move in packs of up to 1.5 million! They are food for lions & tigers. Gnu's are clumsy and noisy.

H is for Himalayan Tahr

LOOK, SEE, and read the facts', exploring is where it's at:

Himalayan Tahr's live at high altitudes in the spring & summer, but migrate in the fall to lower altitudes. The Female Himalayan Tahr's have shorter horns than the male. The horns of a male Himalayan Tahr can grow over a foot long.

I is for Impala

LOOK, SEE, and read the facts', exploring is where it's at:

Impala's are antelopes, they are very noisy.
Impala's make loud grunts and warning snorts.
Impala's are from Africa. Impala's horns grow 36 inches long.

J is for Jaguarundi

LOOK, SEE, and read the facts', exploring is where it's at:

Jaguarundi's hunt during the day, they are from Central & South America. Jaguarundi's are related to cougars, but cougars are bigger. Jagurundi's have short legs for a feline.

K is for Kinkajou

LOOK, SEE, and read the facts', exploring is where it's at:

A Kinkajou is a rainforest mammal related to coatis, raccoons, oligo's and the ringtail. Kinkajous may be mistaken for monkeys or ferrets, bur are not related to either of them. Kinkajous sleep in family units and groom each other. Kinkajous sleep in tree hollows or in shaded tangles of leaves to avoid direct sunlight. Kinkajou's have short-haired, prehensile tails, which it uses as a fifth hand in climbing. Kinkajou's have scent glands on their bellies, near their mouth and on their throat, which allow them to mark their territory and their travel routes.

L is for Loon

LOOK, SEE, and read the facts', exploring is where it's at:

Loons can dive deep into the water, 200 feet in depth. Loons are called divers in different parts of the world. Loons are a group of aquatic birds found in North America and Northern Eurasia.

M is for Mastodon

LOOK, SEE, and read the facts', exploring is where it's at:

Mastodons appear to be similar to elephants and mammoths, but they are not closely related. Mastodon skulls are larger than mammoths and they became extinct about 11,000 years ago.

N is for Nautilus

LOOK, SEE, and read the facts', exploring is where it's at:

Nautilus are characterized by involute or slightly evolute shells that are generally smooth, with compressed or depressed whorl sections straight to sinous sutures, and a tubular. The mouth of a nautilus consists of parrot-like beak made up of two interlocking jaws. You can tell the difference between the male & female by examining the arrangement of tentacles around the buccal.

O is for Orca

LOOK, SEE, and read the facts', exploring is where it's at:

The Orca is known as the killer whale, they are found in the ocean. Orca's can eat more than 500 pounds of food a day and they sometimes hunt and eat sharks and other types of whales. Orca's swim in groups called pods up to 34 miles per hour. Orca's are a type of dolphin, they are the largest.

P is for Praying Mantis

LOOK, SEE, and read the facts', exploring is where it's at:

It has been discovered that after a female praying mantis mate, they may eat their male partner.
Also, the praying mantis has only one ear.

Q is for Quagga

LOOK, SEE, and read the facts', exploring is where it's at:

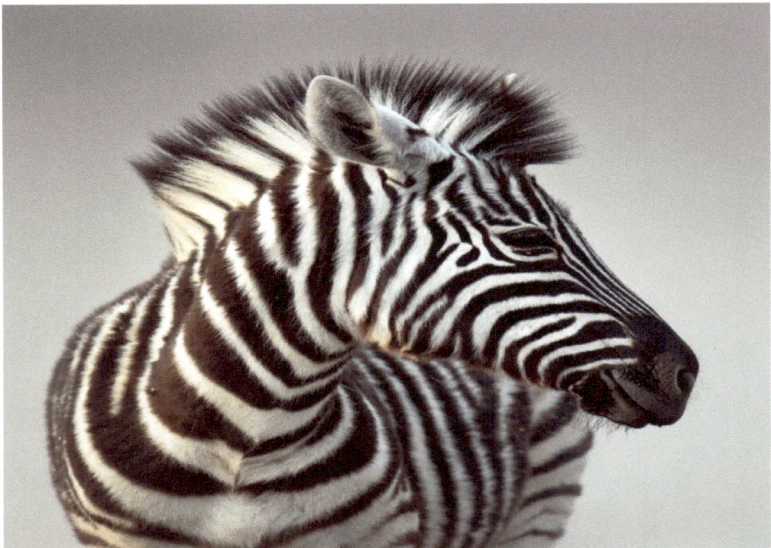

A Quagga is a sub-species of the zebra, which was hunted to extinction in the 19th century. Herds of the Quagga once roamed the plains of southern Africa.

R is for Rhea

LOOK, SEE, and read the facts', exploring is where it's at:

Rhea's are birds native to South America. Rhea's are omnivores. There are two species of Rhea, the Darwin Rhea and the American Rhea. Rhea's are flightless birds.

S is for sea Cucumber

LOOK, SEE, and read the facts', exploring is where it's at:

Sea Cucumbers eat the food particles they extract from mud. See Cucumbers have feeding tenticles around their mouth. Sea Cucumbers discharge sticky, toxic threads to protect them from predators, they have a leathery texture.

T is for Tapir

LOOK, SEE, and read the facts', exploring is where it's at:

Tapirs can grab things with their snout. Tapir's are one of the heaviest land animals and they have erect ears and good hearing. Tapirs are also great swimmers and they are similar to pigs.

U is for Urchin

LOOK, SEE, and read the facts', exploring is where it's at:

Urchins are related to sand dollars, they are protected by their spines. Urchins use there spine as tools to dig into a hiding place. A sea Urchins spine keeps growing so they do not wear away.

V is for Vicuna

LOOK, SEE, and read the facts', exploring is where it's at:

Vicuna's live in high alpine areas of the Andes. Vicunas are the national animal of Peru and the herds are usually led by all females and by a single male. Vicuna's are related to Llama's, Camels and Guanaco's.

W is for Wombat

LOOK, SEE, and read the facts', exploring is where it's at:

Wombat's tails are short and stubby. Wombats are good diggers and generally are solitary.

X is for Xerus

LOOK, SEE, and read the facts', exploring is where it's at:

Xerus, also known as the African Ground Squirrel live in Africa. Xerus eat seeds, insects, fruits, grains and roots. Xerus species are diurnal.

Y is for Yak

LOOK, SEE, and read the facts', exploring is where it's at:

Yaks when domesticated are relied on for milk, meat, wool and sometimes transportation. It is estimated that there are 15,000 yaks remaining in the wild. Yaks live on the bleak, snow swept mountains in the Himalayas.

Z is for Zebu

LOOK, SEE, and read the facts', exploring is where it's at:

It is said that there are 75 known breeds of Zebu. Zebus live in hot climates and are raised in tropical countries.

Below You Will Find A List Of Other Animals In
Alphabetical Order
Challenge Yourself
Look Up And Discover The Amazing Existence Of
Amazing Animals

African Penguin

Burmese

Cuscus

Dwarf Crocodile

Emu

Fur Seal

Grouse

Highland Cattle

Irish Setter

Jellyfish

Kakapo

Lynx

Meerkat

Numbat

Ocelot

Purple Emperor

Quokka

Russian Blue

Sumatron Orangutan

Tapir

Umbrellabird

Vervet Monkey

Wolly Mammoth

X-Ray Tetra

ABC'S OF ANIMALS

ABC'S OF ANIMALS

ABC'S OF ANIMALS

ABC'S OF ANIMALS

ABC'S OF ANIMALS

ABC'S OF ANIMALS

ABC'S OF ANIMALS

ABC'S OF ANIMALS

LIONS: DISCOVER THE SECOND LARGEST LIVING CAT AFTER THE TIGER.

www.ingramcontent.com/pod-product-compliance
Lightning Source LLC
Chambersburg PA
CBHW041817040426
42452CB00001B/5